THE RESILIENT TEACHER

How do I stay positive and effective when dealing with difficult people and policies?

Allen N.
MENDLER

ASCD Alexandria, VA USA

Website: www.ascd.org   www.ascdarias.org
E-mail: books@ascd.org

Printed in the United States of America. Cover art © 2014 by ASCD. ASCD publications present a variety of viewpoints. The views expressed or implied in this book should not be interpreted as official positions of the Association.

PAPERBACK ISBN: 978-1-4166-1943-7   ASCD product #SF114077
Also available as an e-book (see Books in Print for the ISBNs).

Library of Congress Cataloging-in-Publication Data is available for this title. LCCN: 2014018230

21 20 19 18 17 16 15 14   1 2 3 4 5 6 7 8 9 10

THE RESILIENT TEACHER

How do I stay positive and effective when dealing with difficult people and policies?

Want to earn a free ASCD Arias e-book?
Your opinion counts! Please take 2–3 minutes to give
us your feedback on this publication. All survey
respondents will be entered into a drawing to
win an ASCD Arias e-book.

Please visit
www.ascd.org/ariasfeedback

Thank you!

Introduction

Imagine a day when all your students, colleagues, and parents are pleasant, polite, and respectful—they do the important things according to your preferences, and when they disagree, they express themselves without rancor, anger, or attitude. Imagine, too, that you have the freedom to teach your students according to their needs rather than to the dreaded test. If a student misbehaves and you send him to the office, you feel confident that you will get the support you seek; when you speak, your students, colleagues, and administrators really listen. When you call students' parents, they are eager to resolve any issues rather than quick to cast blame at you. Your students are enthusiastic when they enter your room, and so are you. Hard as it may be to believe, *your days can be exactly like this!* Teaching needs to feel satisfying—you owe that to yourself and, more importantly, to your students, who need you to be upbeat, energetic, and inspiring every day to motivate them to do their best.

Being a teacher has never been harder than it has been lately. It is no accident that teacher attrition rates grew by 50 percent between 1993 and 2008 (Kopkowski, 2008). The Common Core State Standards are confusing and ever-shifting. Decisions that affect you every day are being made far beyond your classroom. Students, parents, colleagues, administrators, and unseen state and national officials either don't seem aware of or don't care about the daily realities you face. Whether enshrined in policy or evident in the culture of your school or district, some approaches to teaching kids aren't working, yet few seem willing to do anything about it.

Although there will always be some important issues over which teachers have little control, what you do and say when problems get in the way can often make the difference in achieving, reclaiming, or sustaining the fulfillment you and your students need. In these pages, you will learn how to make rigid policies more flexible, difficult students more cooperative, challenging parents more supportive, and dismissive colleagues more respectful.

The Formula for Happiness

The goal of this book is to enhance your happiness as an educator by providing you:

1. Knowledge of what to say and do when the behavior of your supervisor(s), students, their parents, or your colleagues is interfering with your ability to teach or the ability of your students to learn.

2. Confidence to convincingly express your thoughts and expectations to your students, colleagues, and parents.

3. Influence in being able to do what you think is best even in the face of disagreeable policies or curricula when teaching your students or managing their behavior.

Put simply, *happiness = knowledge + confidence + influence.*

Satisfaction can be hard to achieve. If you try to change everything at once, you'll often change nothing and end up anxious, frustrated, and angry. Remember that you are far more likely to get what you want when you give others what they need—a win-win situation. In the ensuing pages, you will find strategies for implementing change that will give you the confidence you need to take action when obstacles get in the way.

Preventive Maintenance: Six Attitudes That Promote Happiness

If you are unsatisfied at work, start by conducting an internal reality check. You may be missing moments of potential fulfillment simply because you aren't paying close enough attention. Pick a random day and make a list of everything that goes *right* at work, including things that you tend to overlook (e.g., the custodian left the classroom floors nice and shiny, five students actually did their homework, no parents called to complain about anything, Maurice had one temper tantrum instead of his usual three). Making these kinds of lists regularly will help you to embrace the following six attitudes that are guaranteed to enhance your happiness.

1. Be grateful. I think at the core of so much unhappiness is the expectation that we somehow deserve better than we have—better behaved students, better equipped classrooms, more supportive administrators, more realistic standards. Here's a tip: The next time you hear yourself thinking "I deserve [*blank*]," change the formulation to "It would be nice if I had [*blank*], but I appreciate all that I *do* have."

Gratitude is the quickest route to feeling fulfilled, especially when you're sad, angry, or feel unappreciated. In reality, we educators have a pretty amazing life. Most of us have plenty of vacation time and get a chance to affect the lives of young people every day. Although we have a very challenging job, there is much for which to feel thankful. At least once a week, try to set aside 10 minutes to count your blessings. For example, you might reserve time on Friday afternoons to e-mail yourself a list of five things for which you're thankful that week—a list that you make a point to read first thing Monday morning.

2. Sweat the small stuff. Doing little things for others without expecting anything in return helps to build goodwill and encourages others to reciprocate. Offering an appreciative comment or a caring gesture takes little time and has no cost yet can have a profound effect on others. Consider for example the following letter to the editor I recently came across in my local newspaper:

> I was having a very emotional time sitting in the supermarket trying to write a grocery list. I have lost six loved ones in the last two months, and all

of a sudden I just broke down and started crying. I didn't realize anyone was watching me. When I was leaving the store, a total stranger stopped me and gave me a bouquet of flowers and a hug and told me that she would keep me in her prayers. It was like a miracle! I spent the rest of my weekend full of gratitude and crying tears of happiness.

Opportunities for showing students, colleagues, and parents that they matter abound. A caring touch to the shoulder of an unhappy child, a moment spent listening to a stressed colleague, a phone call home to share good news—such small, thoughtful actions are the currency of greater satisfaction because of the affection and cooperation that they can engender. Isn't it easier to like the kids in your class who act friendly and interested? Aren't you more apt to consider joining a committee when approached by a friendly colleague? Be determined to smile, nod, or say hello to everyone you encounter at least one day a week. On other days, commit to approaching at least one person you wouldn't usually reach out to and initiating a social interaction that lasts for at least one minute. Make these gestures part of your daily routine.

3. Make having fun a part of your job. If you need to justify having fun on the job, you'll find plenty of research articles and testimonials online showing the many benefits of a fun workplace, from increased productivity to better health. For teaching to feel satisfying, I believe that work needs to feel playful at least 25 percent of the time. If you are fortunate enough to be at a school with open-minded administrators who put a premium on teacher satisfaction, you probably already have many opportunities to inject some playfulness into your work. If you are at a more formal institution, at the very least make a point of integrating fun stories or personal experiences into your daily instructional routines.

If you are not naturally easygoing, you might get quickly annoyed at students who try to get attention by acting silly. Hard as it might be for you, try to appreciate your class cut-ups a bit more—their levity can lead to a more relaxed and engaging atmosphere. Consider setting aside a few minutes every day or a few times a week for kids to tell jokes or otherwise try to get a laugh (within limits, of course). See what happens to your energy and that of the people around you when you open up your classroom to some refreshing silliness.

4. Challenge yourself to get better. No matter how good you might be at something, you can always get better. I have often seen malaise set in among veteran teachers who do the same thing over and over; many of them develop a defeatist mind-set about their students, schools, or communities, throwing up their hands at problems that they deem unfixable. You can short-circuit such attitudes by meeting and mastering new challenges regularly. The simplest way to start is to identify small, daily, achievable goals. Here are a few examples:

- I am going to spend at least five minutes with Justin before class to make sure he is prepared to answer at least one question correctly during the lesson.
- I am going to introduce one new fact or an old fact in a new way.
- Even though it's not my usual style, I am going to allow Wandering Wendy and Hyperactive Harlan to stand while doing seatwork to see if that improves their concentration.
- I will express at least two positive comments to Oppositional Owen.

5. When you say it, mean it. Be firm about requiring polite and respectful behavior among your students. Let them know from the first day that for them to succeed in your class, they will need to always ask themselves whether what they're about to say is *kind* and whether it is *necessary* before they speak. When students don't obey, confront them firmly and consistently. Move close to the offending student, make solid eye contact, and in a no-nonsense tone explain that what he or she said was either unkind or unnecessary. You might also suggest a more polite way for the student to get his or her point across.

6. Try to surround yourself with at least a few fans. It is virtually impossible to survive, much less actively enjoy, teaching without a support network. Teaching is tough for even the greatest teachers, so it can be immensely helpful and potentially career-saving to maintain a network of supportive colleagues whom you can seek out to remind you of your value on chaotic or exceptionally difficult days.

The suggestions and strategies that follow are for addressing those common problems that can cause teacher burnout. If a problem resonates with you, picture the problem happening as clearly as you can and then practice the script. If necessary, modify the words to create language that is best for you.

You may need to use the strategies more than once before becoming comfortable with them. After planning what you will say or do, identify an optimal time and place to implement the strategy—almost always somewhere private—to avoid embarrassing anyone. Since you are asking someone who is doing something that makes you unhappy to change, remember that change can be difficult for just about everyone. You are likely to have the best chance of getting what you want by being private, tactful, firm, and respectful. Realize that you feel strongly about the problems facing you and refrain from speaking out of anger. If you feel anger bubbling up, take a few deep breaths and wait until you feel calmer. Expressions of anger or blame will only make matters worse. Knowing what you want to have happen and preparing for it is key to success.

When Policies Are the Problem

Many teachers are frustrated by school-, district-, or state-mandated policies, especially those that require them to teach according to a prescribed script or method that doesn't work for some or even all students. The teachers may want to try something different but believe they will be criticized and perhaps punished if they step outside the box. If you find yourself in this situation, the first thing you should do is to check with your colleagues or supervisors to make sure that there isn't a more effective way of implementing the policy. If you can't find a more effective way, your best course of action is to show support for the policy, but also to ask for a trial period for trying a different approach. The following five-step process that can get you the support you seek to sidestep a problematic policy:

1. Begin by identifying and expressing examples of the policy's effectiveness.

2. Identify the students for whom the policy is a barrier to success.

3. Suggest an alternative approach.

4. Express why you think your alternative approach might work better than the original policy, or simply ask permission to implement it.

5. Ask for support during the trial period, which should last at least two (and preferably three) weeks so that you can properly assess the effectiveness of the alternative policy.

You can easily address all five steps in a single statement. Here's an example:

I understand the policy and I think it can work under the right circumstances. [*Offer an example of the policy's effectiveness.*] In most cases, I can see why it should be followed exactly the way it is. Unfortunately, with this [*class/group/student*], I think we would make more progress if we could modify things just a bit. Let me tell you what I have in mind: [*explain why you think your approach would improve on the original*]. I'd like to try it this way for a few weeks and see how it goes. I can't promise that it'll work any better than the original policy, but I'd like to find out. Can I count on your support during this time?

When You Propose an Alternative Approach and It's Rejected

Ask what there is to lose by trying a different approach for a short time when the current policy isn't working. If objections persist and no solid alternatives are proposed, assure those who continue to resist that you will do your best to make the alternative approach work with the kids that you have. Invite skeptical colleagues to visit your class and help you to implement the original policy successfully; unless they are confident that they can show you how to make it work, they will most likely assent to a trial run of an alternative approach:

I wish you felt differently, but I will make every effort to make the current policy work. Thanks for taking the time to give my proposal some thought. I wonder if you wouldn't mind visiting my class and showing me how I might implement the policy more effectively. When can I count on your help?

When You Don't Get the Support You Need From Above

Unfortunately, there are bound to be times when you can't get the support you need. In these cases, you can sometimes make a difference by more clearly expressing what you want. For example, what do you want administrators to do when you send a student to the office? What kind of feedback do you find helpful following an observation? The clearer you are in stating your goals, the more likely you are to get the type of support you are looking for. Here are a few examples:

- When you are watching me teach, I would especially appreciate your comments on the organization and flow of the lesson because I have been working really hard on those aspects of my teaching.

- I try hard not to have kids leave class, even when they misbehave. But when I do, it's because I'm frustrated and need relief, and so do the other students. If we can get together after class and brainstorm alternative options for dealing with difficult students, that would be great; for now, though, when I send a kid out of class, keep in mind that it's because I'm looking for a much-needed time-out.

- Most of my students respond very well to the reward system but some don't. For the next week or so, I'd like to depart a bit from the script and try a new approach. What do you think?

- I just wanted to give you a heads up that Abdul's mother, Ms. Zuchir, seemed upset when I told her that he hasn't been doing his work. She told me that he doesn't like being in my class. When I asked what I could do differently to make school better for him, she insisted that he needs to be in a different class. I would hate to see him moved, but I can live with whatever you decide is best for him.

When You're Expected to Differentiate Among Students with Different Skill Levels, But the Mandated Test Is the Same for All

Think of a test as the finish line of a race that your students are running: They all want to get to the same place, but they may need different training regimens to get there. Here's how to explain this type of approach to stakeholders:

To students: My goal is for all of you to be successful. Success means improving every day. Getting better isn't the same for everyone: Some of us may start out better than others at playing basketball, while others might be quicker than the rest to learn new words. We all start out being good at certain things and maybe not so good at other things, but everyone can get better. [*Here, give examples of people who have improved at certain tasks.*]

Let's say an assignment requires you to come up with a short story. In my class, if I know you can already write a one-page story pretty easily, I might ask you to write two pages instead so that you can be challenged and improve your skills. But if writing is tough for you, I might ask you to only write two sentences and make an audio recording of the rest of your story. At the end of the year, on the state writing test, you will be expected to write a two-page story—but all *I* expect is for you to get better at writing every day. If you do, you won't have to worry about the test.

To administrators and curriculum specialists: I wish I could use the [*curriculum/method/program*] as it is with *all* my kids—that would make my life a lot easier. If you could show me how, I would really appreciate it because unfortunately, I find that some kids are becoming turned off and discouraged. I know the state test requires a two-page story, and my minimum *long-term* goal is for every student to be able to produce one. To achieve that goal, however, I have a *daily* goal for all my students to experience success with writing so that they can see themselves progressing. I know that more of them will have a better chance of passing the test this way. Wouldn't you agree?

To yourself: I can't control what the state requires. Sometimes it's unclear what is required besides getting students' scores up. I'll do my best, but I will not sacrifice either my own or my students' well-being. I need to remind myself that the only way to really get my kids to do better is to get them excited about learning, and the only way to do *that* is by maintaining my energy and optimism. I need to continuously focus on challenging both myself and my students to do better each day. When improvement doesn't happen, I'll see this as analogous to a baseball player having a bad game rather than a bad career. Tomorrow is a new day and a new game.

When Supervisors and Colleagues Are the Problem

When Somebody Takes Credit for Your Work

It sometimes happens that colleagues take credit for work that you've done or they neglect to acknowledge your contributions. If you are enjoying the benefits of the work, it might not be worth the hassle just to get recognized, especially if you have already established a good reputation. You know the contribution you made, so feel good about that. Most people recognize when someone is grandstanding, so it's usually best to avoid raising the issue in public, although it would be reasonable to say something along the following lines:

> It feels good to know that we were able to achieve [*the work*]. The result makes me feel that the time [*names of all involved, including you*] put in was well worth the effort.

If the recognition is very important to you, approach the person who took credit and say the following:

> We both know that I contributed heavily to the work, and it is important to me that I receive proper credit. I worked very hard on our project, and I enjoyed working with you, but when you shared what we did together it seemed like you took credit and forgot to acknowledge my contribution. I would like it if you clarified matters at our next faculty meeting, or if you'd prefer, I can. Which would you rather?

When You Want to Tell Someone to "Take a Hike" But Don't Want to Get in Trouble

There may be times when you want to tell somebody where to go and how quickly to get there, but doing so is almost always a recipe for escalation that will rarely leave you satisfied. The good news is that you can get your point across diplomatically without incurring any consequences. The following approach will almost always give you the upper hand because the recipient is usually unsure of what to say or do next. Teachers who have used this approach often report a major change for the better in the recipient's behavior. Calmly and unemotionally, approach your colleague and make the following statement:

> I don't know if you meant it this way, but what you said/did came across to me as [*pick one: disrespectful, a putdown, something I would never expect to hear from someone in your position or with your background/character/thoughtfulness*]. Is that how you meant it, or did I misunderstand?

The person on the receiving end of such a statement is usually taken aback by the dissonance between the positive traits and hurtful behavior described. More often than not, the response is either, "No, I didn't mean it that way—sorry!" or "No, I meant to say . . ." followed by more respectful feedback.

When You Are Being Bullied by Your Administrator or Supervisor

The vast majority of school leaders are caring educators who treat staff with respect and dignity. Sadly, however, there are always exceptions. Here are just a few of the comments I've heard about supervisors from competent teachers at schools I have visited:

- He made me feel like I was a useless teacher.
- She smiles to my face but behind my back she says things that make me look bad.
- My kids get high test scores and I consistently have good relationships with them, but I don't get as much

as a "hello" from the principal when he passes me in the hall.

- I would go home at night with a knot in my stomach. I dreaded walking past the office on my way to my classroom, never knowing when "the rattlesnake" might attack.
- One day I walked into my classroom and everything that made my room special was removed. I couldn't believe she would do that.

Unfortunately, there is no easy way to get someone who has more power to stop bullying you. In general, it is best not to ignore the bullying and to work to defuse it as best you can. If the bullying persists, you may need to use whatever district, union, or legal resources are available. You might be able to make yourself less of a target by not feeding the power sought by the perpetrator. Avoid engaging in debate when criticized. Keep a log of incidents, including dates, times, and descriptions of the offenses. I know of one teacher who pulled out her phone, hit record, and said to her tormentor, "You wouldn't mind repeating those comments and suggestions to help me remember, would you?" At that, the supervisor abruptly stopped and left. Robert Mueller, author of *Bullying Bosses* (2005), suggests what he calls the Restroom Retreat: Excuse yourself to use the restroom while the bully is still talking. Doing this sends a clear message that you won't tolerate the abuse.

One way to defuse verbal aggression is by calmly disagreeing or simply acknowledging that the other person has spoken. Repeatedly disrupting the bully's momentum in this way can lessen your chances of remaining a target. Here are a few examples of simple yet effective interjections you might use:

- I don't see it that way.
- That's your opinion, not mine.
- I don't appreciate being talked about in that way.
- I'm sorry you feel that way.
- You seem really angry/frustrated/annoyed.

If the bullying continues regardless, recognize that the perpetrator probably has a personality disorder and is best avoided. If he or she tries to bait you in public, keep your comments brief, limit-setting, and assertive (e.g., "That was inappropriate."). Stay away from emotional words like *hurtful* and try not to display strong emotion, since doing so merely gives the bully the power and drama that he or she seeks.

When You Are Singled Out in Front of Your Colleagues

Nobody likes negative feedback, but some people are uncomfortable even receiving positive feedback from colleagues; they either think what they did was no big deal or they don't want to invite resentment from others who haven't been recognized. Here are examples of ways to address negative and positive feedback in front of others:

- For negative feedback: [*Wait until you have a private moment with the person before proceeding.*] Your feedback is important to me and I know I have a lot to learn, but I don't appreciate being corrected in public. If there is a next time, please wait until you can share that kind of feedback privately. Thank you.

- For positive feedback: Thanks for the positive feedback. While we're at it, I think Mrs. Jones deserves recognition for her contributions as well.

When You Send Kids to the Office for Misbehavior, But No Consequences Are Forthcoming

For the most part, administrators are no more successful at fixing student misbehavior than anyone else. Your best bet is to use the office as you might a colleague—that is, for short-term relief. I would strongly suggest that you develop a small network of colleagues that you can count on to let you have a break from students whose behavior significantly interferes with teaching and learning. Let your administrator know that you will do everything you can to avoid sending a student out of your classroom, but when you do, you are primarily asking for relief because the student has made it impossible for you to teach at that moment. Specify how much time away from the student you need (or the student needs) for things to proceed more smoothly. You should rarely ask for more than 15 minutes. Be sure to meet with your administrator before the school year begins to lay out a workable plan. Here's an example of how to ask for support from administrators:

I'd like you to take a look at the rules and consequences I have posted in my classroom.

Rarely do I send kids to the office, but when I do it's either because the student is so disruptive that it is impossible for me to teach or because I need some time away from the student's irritating behavior. If I send the student to you with a blue referral slip, I'm looking for a 15-minute break. A yellow slip means something more serious has happened—if a student has one of those, please hold onto him or her until I have a chance to see you. I would really appreciate that. Does that work for you?

If you think there is a certain action or consequence that you think would be more effective, let the administrator know as follows:

Thank you so much for helping me out with Ernesto. I really appreciate your support. Should I need your help again, and I hope it won't, I think doing [*identify what you think might work better*] with Ernesto would work best—that's just my hunch based on my knowledge of his circumstances.

When You Are Criticized in Front of Your Students

It is extremely important that you handle criticism in front of students immediately. You cannot afford to be undermined in front of your students; it diminishes your authority and can lead to undesirable consequences. As soon as possible, seek a private moment, and say something like this:

Although your feedback is important, I don't appreciate being corrected in front of my students. I'm sure you didn't mean to, but it undermines my authority and I can't have that. In the future, when you have something to say, I would really appreciate getting your feedback privately. Can I count on that?

When Colleagues Gossip or Put People Down

Redirect the conversation to make it more productive. Gossip and putdowns are usually expressions of frustration. Those who engage in them are either letting off steam or too proud to ask for the help that they need. One strategy is to express your disapproval and then ask a question that gives the other person an opportunity for reflection. Here's an example: "I don't find it helpful to talk about Mary in that way. Are you just letting off steam or are you looking for some way to improve things?" After hearing the other person's answer, offer a supportive comment (e.g., "Sometimes I need to let off steam too, especially when I haven't found a solution to a sticky problem.") or an example from your own experience that might be helpful (e.g., "For what it's worth, when I force myself to think of a 'lazy' student as someone who doesn't try because he is afraid to fail, I feel less frustrated and more ready to try to find a solution. If you want to brainstorm some possibilities either now or in the future, let me know.").

When Student Behavior Is the Problem

When Students Say That You Can't Tell Them What to Do

It's best to deal with oppositional behavior by acknowledging the student's need for control without surrendering yours. Unless you want to get into a power struggle, your best bet is to agree by reminding the student that, ultimately, only he has the power to control his behavior (e.g., "You're right: Only you can make yourself do the right thing, and I hope you will."). If the problem continues, don't be tempted to escalate your demand (e.g., "Put the phone away right now!"). Instead, offer the student an opportunity to save face by letting him know that it's probably best to avoid a power struggle (e.g., "You know, it might be a good idea to put your cell phone away in order to avoid a hassle that might make one or both of us uncomfortable. Thanks for your cooperation."). Then redirect your attention away from the student by returning to the lesson or calling on another student. If the problem persists, meet individually with the student, explain the problem with his behavior, and invite him to offer a workable solution:

> There are school rules about cell phones that you aren't following. If this behavior continues, I will

have no choice but to write you up [*or call home, nag you, take the phone away*], but I would prefer to work this out between us. So, how can we fix the problem?

If the student complains about school policies, explain why they are needed or defer to a higher authority:

I like the rule because I think cell phones are a distraction from the kind of learning that needs to happen in this class. But if you are unhappy with the rule and feel strongly that it should be changed, there are some ways you can go about it properly. Because this rule was made by school administrators [*or district or state officials*], they are the ones you'll need to convince that it should be changed. Until that happens, I'll need you to follow the rule. Let me know if you feel strongly enough about it, and if so, I'll try to share some ways for you to get your voice heard.

When Students Don't Listen or Seem to Ignore You

Good listening is a skill that needs to be learned, so have your students practice it. Give them a discussion topic, have them pair up, and ask each student to paraphrase what her partner says. The speaker has to feel that the listener understands her before the two can switch roles.

Some students expect adults to endlessly repeat things. Let your students know early on that you will rarely repeat directions. When you do give directions or express your expectations, ask a reliable student to summarize what you've said. Then, have students pair up and paraphrase your words to each other before continuing. If confusion persists, tell students that they need to ask at least three other students for clarification before asking you.

If you have asked a student to behave better and he doesn't respond appropriately, try saying something along these lines:

> Brad, I asked you to [*identify the proper behavior*] and you haven't yet. Did you not hear me, or are you choosing to continue breaking the rules? I hope you just didn't hear me and you will now do the right thing. Thanks.

After you say this, change the focus back to the lesson even if the student does not comply. If the student attempts to escalate the discussion, refuse. Postpone any disciplinary action unless the student is making it hard for you to teach (e.g., "I hope you can quickly [*identify the proper behavior*] so that it won't be necessary for you to go to the office, because I will miss you if you go, even though right now I am not happy with the choice you are making. Try to stay with us if it is at all possible!")

When You See Students from Other Classes Behaving Inappropriately

If you don't know the student by name, approach her with a made-up one and politely but firmly tell her what you want. Calling students by a name—even the wrong one—tends to make them less combative. Here's an example:

Teacher: Excuse me, Joelle.

Student: My name's not Joelle, it's Riley.

Teacher: Oops! Sorry, Riley. I noticed you must have accidentally forgotten to [*identify the proper behavior*]. Thanks for fixing it right now/ remembering to do so next time.

When Students Don't Complete Homework

Homework assignments should be reserved for practice, review, and application rather than new learning. Let your students know the purpose and rationale for each assignment. For example, perhaps you want to know how well your students have learned a certain concept. Explain why you are giving them the assignment and what you expect them (or you) to get out of it. Let them know approximately how long the assignment should take to complete. Students should be able to do their homework with minimal assistance, and each assignment should take them no more than five minutes per grade level to complete (and preferably less). If it takes them longer, you need to know so that you can make adjustments.

Here are some examples of how to talk to students who haven't completed their homework:

- Maria, I assigned last night's homework so I could get an idea of how much more practice some of us might need. Maybe I didn't make that clear. Now that you know, when can I expect to see your completed assignment?

- Carlos, even champions need practice to get better, and I expect you to act like a champion. When do you plan to start?
- Todd, if I see at least three of your homework questions answered correctly, I promise I won't waste your time by giving you more of the same some other night. Is that a deal?

Here are a few additional tips related to homework:

- Instead of giving kids negative consequences when they don't do their homework, offer them positive incentives when they do (e.g., an A or feedback that will help them to earn an A).
- Have students start their homework in class, and check to make sure that they're all on the right track before they leave.
- Differentiate assignments so that each student concentrates on areas needing improvement.
- Don't assign homework every night; instead, assign it well in advance. Let students know when the homework is due, and in the meantime, offer them occasional reminders along with opportunities to get help if they need it.

When You Know There Will Be a Substitute Teacher

Let your students know that they will have a substitute teacher and that you expect them to behave properly. You might consider offering them a special reward if they behave well for the substitute, especially if they are usually very challenging. Don't tell them what the reward is—the surprise factor will keep them on their toes. Then, in private, approach the most challenging students in your class and tell them that you especially want to hear positive things about them and you expect them to help the substitute make things go smoothly. Here's an example:

> I intend to give you a call after school tomorrow to hear how things went, and I expect to hear good things. You guys are class leaders and I am counting on you, so don't let me down. Do whatever you can to make sure that things go smoothly and there are no problems. Are you up to it?

When Students Complain or Are Unresponsive

Let your students know statements such as "I can't," "this is stupid," "this is too hard," and "I don't know" are banned from your classroom unless the words *yet, so far,* or *up until now* are appended to them. Here are some examples:

- I can't do those math problems *yet.*
- This book is really stupid *up until now.*
- This class is boring *so far.*
- That essay is too hard *up until now.*
- I don't know *yet.*

Motivation is easier to sustain when challenges are viewed as temporary rather than permanent.

Some students resort to repeatedly saying "I don't know" as a way of getting adults to back off. Consider the following example:

> Teacher: Max, why did you get in trouble at lunch?
> Max: I don't know. I wasn't doing anything.
> Teacher: You must have done something. What was it?
> Max: I don't know.
> Teacher: Am I going to have to ask the lunch lady what happened?
> Max: I don't know.

A more effective approach would be to respond to the student's first "I don't know" with something along these lines: "Probably lots of things were going on, Max. If you did know, what would you say?" Here are some other effective responses to common student phrases:

- For "I wasn't doing anything": If you *were* doing something, what would it have been? (Or, If I asked the lunch lady what you were doing, what do you think she would say?)
- For "I don't care": If you *did* care, what would you do or say differently?
- For "You can't make me": You are right. How can you make yourself [*identify the appropriate behavior*]?
- For "You're always picking on me": I guess I must miss what some of the other kids are doing. I'll try harder not to, but if I do it again, what can you do differently if you don't want trouble?

When Students Give Up Easily or Seem Determined to Fail

This is not usually an easy problem to fix. Here are three steps you can take to help your students persevere:

1. Take some ownership for the student's failure. Example: "I let you down. I should have helped you more, and I didn't. I am disappointed in myself, and we are going to fix this. If you prepare, plan, and practice correctly, you can pass this class, and I will help you."

2. Build confidence by telling the student what you plan to do and what she needs to do. Example: "I've done a lot of teaching, so I know what we need to do. I'll prepare some extra material and we'll spend some special time practicing. I expect you to join me!"

3. Encourage the student by celebrating her successes during practice. Example: "You got this, this, and that correct. Way to go!"

When a Problem Persists, But You Don't Have a Good Way to Address It

"Let's see, should I send the kid to the office, call his parents, keep him after school, or move him to red? Heck, I've already done all that and none of it works!" Sometimes you are stuck with the limited options you have, in which case I suggest picking the least undesirable path while also committing to seek a better solution. Here's an example:

Jose, I don't know what to do when you lash out like this. I can't let you hurt others. I know it sometimes helps to take a few deep breaths and a quick walk. If you can do that more often to calm yourself, that would be great, because I hate sending you to the time-out room. When you are there, you are missing the lesson, and I miss you being with us. Can you think of some other things you could do to calm down?

If the student doesn't offer an alternative, conclude with a statement along the following lines: "Let's keep getting together like we are right now. If you think of something better that can keep you in class when you get upset, please let me know, and I'll do the same."

When Parents Are the Problem

When Parents Are Doing Their Children's Schoolwork

Be sure to assign homework that students can at least begin to work on successfully in class. Because parents are motivated to do their kids' work by the prospect of higher grades, another effective solution is to check for homework completion, not grade it.

At every opportunity, be sure to let parents know that you value effort over achievement. Tell them how long they should expect their children to work on assignments at home;

if their kids take longer or seem especially frustrated, invite them to notify you so that you can pursue the matter. Here's an example of how to address these issues with parents:

> The homework I assign is intended for practice or review. Sometimes I want to see if my students can apply what I've taught them. Homework is as much for me as it is for the students; it's a way for me to check to see if they need more help. You might expect your kids to ask you the occasional question that you can quickly answer, but if they keep asking, or if you notice that you are starting to act like a teacher, please stop. Instead, let me know so I can figure out how to best teach your child.

When Parents Excuse Their Children's Irresponsible Behavior

No parent wants to purposely raise an irresponsible child. Many simply find it easier to avoid fighting with their kids when they make a fuss. When students behave poorly and their parents make excuses for them, you will want to speak to the parents' sense of pride in raising a respectful and responsible child. Here's an example:

> I would be letting Susie down if I didn't expect her to better manage her anger, and I won't do that. I have too much respect for her to lower my expectations. Further, I am sure you agree that we all need to get her to understand that being responsible means managing her anger, even if it isn't always easy to do

so and even if she isn't the only one at fault. I would really appreciate your support on this matter, but more important is to let Susie know that we expect better from her. Does that make sense?

If the parents persist in defending their child, ask them if they can tell you what works for them at home when the child misbehaves.

When Parents Blame You for Their Child's School-Related Problems

When parents tell you that their child finds your class boring, blames you for his poor performance, or accuses you of picking on him, start by acknowledging their concerns. Then remind them about your goals and invite them to offer some strategies that you might use to help their child overcome his problems. Here's an example:

I am glad you are letting me know these concerns because I want to be the best teacher possible for your child. I can assure you that I am not trying to pick on him. My goal is for him to be successful in school, but maybe I'm not going about it in the right way. Can you give me some tips on how I might get this point across to him without making him feel like I'm picking on him?

When Parents Threaten to Report You to a Higher Authority

If you know that your classroom decisions are grounded in sound educational thinking, stick to your convictions. You should never feel forced to do anything you believe to be ethically wrong. You are on solid footing if your decision is based on what you believe to be best for the student. Here are some steps to take when parents say that they'll take their concerns to administrators:

1. Reflect on the parents' frustration.

2. Acknowledge that there are other ways to look at things.

3. Point out how much you appreciate the deep caring that the parents are demonstrating.

4. Hold firm to your decision.

5. Keep your door open.

6. Alert administrators that one of your students' parents might contact them soon.

Here's an example of how to negotiate a discussion with parents who say they'll report you:

> I know you aren't hearing me say what you'd like, and I know that it doesn't feel good. You have strong feelings about this issue, and while we don't see things the same way on this, I have a lot of respect for you. Your child is very lucky to have a parent

who cares so deeply. If you think discussing this issue with the principal is necessary, I hope you'll do that. In fact, I'll let him know that you might be calling. Thanks for coming in and letting me know your concerns.

Problems That Cross Categories

When You Are Blindsided by Feedback

One day early in my career, as I was busy tucking things away for the summer, I had a parent show up in my classroom unannounced. Despite my repeated requests to meet with her, this was the first time she set foot in the classroom.

"I just want to say that you are the worst excuse for a teacher I know," she said. "Did you enjoy making my child feel miserable all year long?"

With that, she abruptly turned and left without waiting for an answer. I was completely dumbfounded; I had no idea that she felt this way, and I felt I had let her child down. A few days later I called the parent to discuss things further, and I was prepared to apologize for whatever I might have done to upset her. Although she never answered the phone, the experience taught me to be more proactive about seeking feedback from administrators, students, and parents. Here are some ways of seeking feedback from others so that you're not blindsided by criticism:

- *For administrators:* I do the best I can every day to help my students be successful and responsible. If it ever comes to your attention that I can do better or if you notice things I am doing to achieve those goals, I hope you will let me know. I value your feedback.
- *For parents:* Your child's learning and success are most important to me. If you have concerns at any time, please let me know. I also like to hear when you feel good about your child's experience in my class. I answer all e-mail messages received by 3 p.m. on the same day. If you want to speak to me directly, I am available on [*day of the week*] at [*timeframe*].
- *For students:* For homework tonight, I'd like you to write two things I am doing to help you be successful in this class, and two things I could be doing better to help you be even more successful.

Because emotion often takes over when you are blindsided, it is best to postpone your response until you have had a chance to clear your head and review the situation. Otherwise, you might say or do something that you'll later regret. Begin by saying something along the lines of, "Wow! You caught me by surprise" or "I had no idea you felt that way." Then, tell the other person that you realize it is very important that you discuss what is bothering him or her. Ask if the other person can think of a good time to meet and talk some more about things, or suggest a time to meet that allows you to be emotionally prepared beforehand. Alternatively, you could simply say, "I'm speechless right now, but I'll get back to you when I know what I want to say."

When You Have a Gut Feeling That Something Isn't Right but You Just Can't Figure Out What It Is

Perhaps a student or colleague is being short-tempered. Maybe a student is restless or disengaged and you don't know why. When something doesn't feel right consider saying the following:

> You seem [*distant/upset/sad/worried*]. I wonder if I did or said something that I'm not aware of or if there's something else that might be bothering you. Can you help me understand what's going on and how I might help?

When You Blow It and You Know It

We all say or do things that we regret. You will feel better about yourself and usually get a positive reaction if you apologize directly and sincerely to the offended party. If your offense was in public, the apology should be, too; otherwise, it's best to apologize in private. Here's an idea of how to phrase your apology:

> I blew it! I am really sorry that I [*name the offense*]. That wasn't right and I should've known better. There are no excuses. I know I got overly emotional, and I apologize for that. I am sorry if I was hurtful.

If you think that the other party is also at least partly at fault, you can add, "Now that you know what I wish I had done differently, is there anything you think you could have done differently to keep us both from getting so upset?"

If the person seems unaware, share something specific: "For what it is worth, I am more likely to change things when I am asked in private at the end of class. If you can remember to talk privately in the future, I would appreciate it."

It can be especially powerful if you apologize without even knowing precisely what, if anything, you may have done wrong:

> I want to apologize to you because I know I must have done or said something that bothers you given how you're acting. I'd like to make things better, but I'm not sure how. What happened that made you so upset?

When You're Bummed Out and Overwhelmed Because Your Kids' Problems Outweigh Your Ability to Deal with Them

If you are a caring person, you will occasionally become discouraged by challenges that originate and persist outside school. At these times, it is essential to remind yourself that when you retain a sense of hope and belief in yourself and your students, your active presence in their lives can make a real difference. Like a seeds that require regular watering before they sprout, some students need lots of nurturing before they grow. With that in mind, here are some examples of what to think, say, and do that can help you to sustain or reclaim optimism:

- Remember the story of the boy on the beach who tosses a starfish that had washed ashore back into the ocean. Sad that he couldn't toss back the many other starfish that had also washed ashore, the boy asked a wise man what difference it made to save only one among so many. The wise man told the boy that to the starfish he threw back, he made all the difference in the world.
- You may not be able to do everything, but you can always do something.
- Seek to achieve one or two small goals every day. Here are some examples:
  - Get Bethany to smile at least twice.
  - Find two reasons to give Jared a high five or a fist bump.
  - Ask Tanisha why she has been absent lately, tell her you've missed her, and ask her if there's anything you can do to help.
  - Give 150 percent during school time—and then focus on yourself.

A Final Strategy

So, what happens if you try out all of the suggestions in these pages and you still don't feel satisfied? Some years ago, my wife, who was a special education coordinator, counseled a very bright young man out of the teaching profession. He was an adequate teacher, but he just didn't enjoy it. His lessons were emotionless and he was often sarcastic with students and colleagues. In his spare time, this young man would spend hours blissfully tinkering in his garage. After considerable reflection, he decided to quit teaching and ended up becoming an extraordinarily successful salesman of construction products, eventually opening his own business. To this day, he thanks my wife for encouraging him to find what he really wanted to do and go for it. Perhaps you should as well. There is no shame in finding what makes you truly happy and productive—life, after all, is short.

If you are committed to remain a teacher, you owe it to yourself and your students to find the fulfillment that has eluded you. To do so, consider the following experiment. Over the course of one month, become an actor for at least two hours per school day. Try to vary your schedule so that every two-hour block of classes gets to experience your act at least once a week. During these two hours, act as though you worked in the greatest school that ever existed, with fabulous colleagues and administrators, policies you agree with, a rich and exciting curriculum, and kids who are motivated to learn and eager to behave. During these two hours, move around with an extra bounce in your step and a welcoming demeanor. At first, your acting might not feel at all natural to you. That's alright—think of the first week as a rehearsal. Think about it: Actors have to put their game faces on no matter how they feel when they perform in a play. Their job is to entertain to

the highest level of their talent. Try the same thing yourself—
act as if you are the most satisfied teacher anywhere. Begin
tomorrow and see what happens.

To give your feedback on this publication and
be entered into a drawing for a free ASCD
Arias e-book, please visit
www.ascd.org/ariasfeedback

ASCD | arias™

ENCORE

A TIP A DAY FOR STAYING POSITIVE AT WORK

To keep up a positive frame of mind, consider the following tips as a daily diet of inspiration. There are approximately 20 school days per month, so you can try a different strategy every day. (Naturally, if some work better for you than others, feel free to make substitutions.)

1. Compliment at least three students with whom you rarely have positive interactions.

2. Initiate a conversation with one of your most challenging students that lasts at least two minutes. Feel free to discuss anything other than discipline or motivation issues. Be sure to share at least one thing about yourself that the student probably doesn't know.

3. Bring a bouquet of flowers to work. Stop to admire them and take in their fragrance at least once every half hour. If you don't like flowers, bring in an object that offers a pleasant aroma instead and take a whiff whenever you feel stressed.

4. Share a feel-good story with each class.

5. Call the parents of at least two of your best students and share good news about their child with them.

6. Call the parents of at least one of your most challenging students and share something positive with them.

7. Change it up. Most of us stand in the same spot or move around in a predictable pattern every day without

even noticing. Get off your spot today: Start each class in a different place, and move to a different spot at least once every five minutes.

8. Forgive yourself each time you start to beat yourself up. When you're stressed, silently repeat the following: "I am doing my best. I can't do everything. I will get through this day."

9. Give yourself a hug. Wrap your arms around yourself and hug yourself as you would a friend in need of nurturing.

10. Place an invisible shield around yourself that allows only positive messages in. Watch anything negative bounce off.

11. Indulge in a loud belly laugh that lasts at least 30 seconds, once in the morning and once after lunch. If you can find someone to join you, great! If not, close your door during a break and start laughing.

12. Devote at least 45 minutes of your lesson today to *fun*. These 45 minutes may or may not have anything to do with the prescribed curriculum. If you can't think of what to do, consult with one or two students for whom having fun appears to come easily (perhaps at your expense).

13. Inform your students that tomorrow they'll be taking a five-minute open-book quiz that all can ace if they just *arrive on time and prepared* (e.g., one to five questions that point students to the specific pages in their textbooks where they can find the answers.)

14. Tell an administrator something you appreciate about him or her (e.g., "I really appreciate how promptly you notify

parents about upcoming events. With all that's on your plate, I know it isn't easy to stay on top of these little but important things.")

15. Thank everybody you interact with *before* you get what you seek (e.g., "Please open your books to page 55. Thanks, Billy." "I know there are going to be some changes to the curriculum as a result of the Common Core standards, Principal Jones, and I'd really appreciate getting a chance to share my thoughts before decisions are finalized. Thanks for the opportunity.")

16. Notice any and all negative emotions (e.g., anger, annoyance, stress, anxiety). Whenever you feel any of these, take a moment to acknowledge them, then let them float away like clouds in the sky.

17. Bring a picture or two of places or people that give you great joy to work. Keep it on your desk or in an easily visible location. Focus your attention on it at least once every 15 minutes, picturing yourself in the picture. Take a moment to relive all the feelings and thoughts that you experience.

18. Enjoy at least one relaxing meal today. If you like to cook and have the time, make the meal from scratch. Savor every bite and sip; let the food fill your mouth as you taste the flavor and feel the texture. At some point, silently say to yourself, "I work hard. I am in a tough situation. I get better results than I usually acknowledge and I deserve to take good care of myself."

19. Sit down during one or more of your breaks today. Close your eyes, drop your head and shoulders, and take

notice of your breathing for a few moments. Breath in deeply and exhale fully. Continue to do this throughout your break. If you experience distracting thoughts, let them float away like puffs of smoke. If you feel tightness or tension in your shoulders, squeeze and release.

20. Unsqueeze your day. Many of us make ourselves tense by trying to squeeze way too much into each day. Today, squeeze *out*—for example, if you would normally try to cover two concepts in the lesson, cover one. If you usually run four errands after school, run three today instead. If asked to add tasks to your day, say "I'm sorry, I can't" instead of "Sure."

Bibliography

Benson J. (2014) *Hanging in: Strategies for teaching the students who challenge us most.* Alexandria, VA: ASCD.

Ciaccio, J. (2004). *Totally positive teaching.* Alexandria, VA: ASCD.

Curwin, R., Mendler, A., & Mendler, B. (2008). *Discipline with dignity: New challenges, new solutions* (3rd. ed.). Alexandria, VA: ASCD.

Kopkowski, C. (2008, April). Why they leave. *NEA Today.* Available: http://www.nea.org/home/12630.htm

Mendler, A. (2000). *Motivating students who don't care.* Bloomington IN: Solution Tree.

Mendler, A. (2001). *Connecting with students.* Alexandria, VA: ASCD.

Mendler, A. (2006). *Handling difficult parents: Successful strategies for educators.* Rochester, NY: Discipline Associates.

Mendler, A. (2012). *When teaching gets tough: Smart ways to reclaim your game.* Alexandria, VA: ASCD.

Mendler, A., & Mendler, B. (2012). *Power struggles: Successful techniques for educators.* Bloomington, IN: Solution Tree.

Mendler, B., Curwin, R., & Mendler, A. (2007). *Strategies for successful classroom management.* Thousand Oaks, CA: Corwin.

Mueller, R. (2005). *Bullying bosses: A survivor's guide.* Publisher: Author.

Related Resources: Teacher Effectiveness

At the time of publication, the following ASCD resources were available (ASCD stock numbers appear in parentheses). For up-to-date information about ASCD resources, go to www.ascd.org. You can search the complete archives of *Educational Leadership* at http://www.ascd.org/el.

ASCD EDge©
Exchange ideas and connect with other educators interested in teacher effectiveness on the social networking site ASCD EDge at http://ascdedge.ascd.org.

Print Products
The 12 Touchstones of Good Teaching: A Checklist for Staying Focused Every Day by Elizabeth Ross Hubbell and Bryan Goodwin (#113009)

Becoming a Better Teacher: Eight Innovations that Work by Giselle Martin-Kniep (#100043)

Changing the Way You Teach, Improving the Way Your Students Learn by Giselle Martin-Kniep and Joanne Picone-Zocchia (#108001)

Connecting with Students by Allen N. Mendler (#101236)

Enhancing Professional Practice: A Framework for Teaching by Charlotte Danielson (#106034)

ASCD PD Online© Courses
Leadership: Effective Critical Skills (#PD09OC08)
The Reflective Educator (#PD11OC114)

For more information: send e-mail to member@ascd.org; call 1-800-933-2723 or 703-578-9600, press 2; send a fax to 703-575-5400; or write to Information Services, ASCD, 1703 N. Beauregard St., Alexandria, VA 22311-1714 USA.

About the Author

Allen N. Mendler is an educator and school psychologist and lives in Rochester, New York. He has worked extensively with children of all ages in general and special education settings. He has consulted for many schools and day and residential centers throughout the world, providing training on classroom management, discipline, and motivating difficult students. As the coauthor of *Discipline with Dignity* (ASCD, 1999) and author of many other publications, Mendler's emphasis is on developing effective frameworks and strategies for educators, youth professionals, and parents to help youth at risk succeed.